# BULLET HOLE

by Gloria Williams

samuelfrench.co.uk

FOR PROFESSIONAL AND AMATEUR PRODUCTION
ENQUIRIES

UNITED KINGDOM AND WORLD
EXCLUDING NORTH AMERICA
plays@samuelfrench.co.uk
020 7255 4302/01

UNITED STATES AND CANADA
info@samuelfrench.com
020 7255 4302/01

Each title is subject to availability from Samuel French,
depending upon country of performance.

# *Acting* Editions

## BORN TO PERFORM

**Playscripts designed from the ground up to work the way you do in rehearsal, performance and study**

---

*Larger*, clearer text for easier reading

*Wider* margins for notes

*Performance features* such as character and props lists, sound and lighting cues, and more

---

## + CHOOSE A SIZE AND STYLE TO SUIT YOU

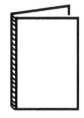

| **STANDARD EDITION** | **SPIRAL-BOUND EDITION** | **LARGE EDITION** |
|---|---|---|
| Our regular paperback book at our regular size | The same size as the Standard Edition, but with a sturdy, easy-to-fold, easy-to-hold spiral-bound spine | A4 size and spiral bound, with larger text and a blank page for notes opposite every page of text – perfect for technical and directing use |

LEARN MORE | **samuelfrench.co.uk/actingeditions**

## MUSIC USE NOTE

Licensees are solely responsible for obtaining formal written permission from copyright owners to use copyrighted music in the performance of this play and are strongly cautioned to do so. If no such permission is obtained by the licensee, then the licensee must use only original music that the licensee owns and controls. Licensees are solely responsible and liable for all music clearances and shall indemnify the copyright owners of the play(s) and their licensing agent, Samuel French, against any costs, expenses, losses and liabilities arising from the use of music by licensees. Please contact the appropriate music licensing authority in your territory for the rights to any incidental music.

## USE OF COPYRIGHT MUSIC

A licence issued by Samuel French Ltd to perform this play does not include permission to use the incidental music specified in this copy.

Where the place of performance is already licensed by the PERFORMING RIGHT SOCIETY (PRS) a return of the music used must be made to them. If the place of performance is not so licensed then application should be made to the PRS, 2 Pancras Square, London, N1C 4AG.

A separate and additional licence from PHONOGRAPHIC PERFORMANCE LTD, 1 Upper James Street, London W1F 9DE (www.ppluk.com) is needed whenever commercial recordings are used.

## IMPORTANT BILLING AND CREDIT REQUIREMENTS

If you have obtained performance rights to this title, please refer to your licensing agreement for important billing and credit requirements.

## ABOUT THE AUTHOR

Gloria Williams is an award-winning British actress and playwright, who is a graduate of The Royal Court Theatre Young Writers' Group and Talawa Theatre Company. She wrote *Bullet Hole* which premiered at the Camden Fringe Festival 2017 and was shortlisted for the Alfred Fagon Choice Award.

Her most notable work to date, *Monday,* garnered widespread acclaim at international festivals. *Monday* was performed at New York's Samuel French Off Broadway One Act Play Festival at The Manhattan Repertory Theatre in Times Square. It premiered in the UK at The Lost One Act Play Festival, winning 'Best Overall Production', as judged by *The Times'* critic, Jeremy Kingston.

## AUTHOR'S NOTE

I have always been passionate about exposing the issues affecting the black community. My first play, *Monday*, explored child abuse in a Black British religious family.

I developed *Bullet Hole* as I believed writing a play about Female Genital Mutilation was a good platform to condemn an old tradition which oppresses women. This brutal practice is still present in our current time, worldwide and is not spoken about enough. I hope that the production serves to raise awareness, using drama as a tool to educate audiences.

*Gloria Williams*
*September 2018*

*Bullet Hole* was first produced by Freedom Tongues & Naiad Productions in association with Park Theatre in Park90, London, on 2 October 2018, with the following cast and creatives:

| | |
|---|---|
| **CLEO** | Gloria Williams |
| **EVE** | Doreene Blackstock |
| **WINNIE** | Anni Domingo |

| | |
|---|---|
| Writer | Gloria Williams |
| Producers | Gloria Williams (Freedom Tongues) |
| | Lara Genovese (Naiad Productions Ltd) |
| Director | Lara Genovese |
| Creative Assistant | Emma Zadow |
| Sound Designer | Ed Clarke |
| Lighting Designer | Rajiv Pattani |
| Designer | Lara Genovese |
| Photography | Naiad Photography |
| Deputy Stage Manager | Ricky McFadden |
| Social Media Marketing | Roberto Landi |

## ABOUT PARK THEATRE

Park Theatre was founded by Artistic Director, Jez Bond and Associate Artistic Director, Melli Marie. The building opened in May 2013 and, with four West End transfers, two National Theatre transfers and ten national tours in its first four years, quickly garnered a reputation as a key player in the London theatrical scene. Park Theatre has received two Olivier nominations, won an Offie for Best New Play (*The Revlon Girl*) and won The Stage's Fringe Theatre of the Year in 2015.

Park Theatre is an inviting and accessible venue, delivering work of exceptional calibre in the heart of Finsbury Park. We work with writers, directors and designers of the highest quality to present compelling, exciting and beautifully told stories across our two intimate spaces.

Our programme encompasses a broad range of work from classics to revivals with a healthy dose of new writing, producing in-house as well as working in partnership with emerging and established producers. We strive to play our part within the UK's theatre ecology by offering mentoring, support and opportunities to artists and producers within a professional theatre-making environment.

Our Creative Learning strategy seeks to widen the number and range of people who participate in theatre, and provides opportunities for those with little or no prior contact with the arts.

In everything we do we aim to be warm and inclusive; a safe, welcoming and wonderful space in which to work, create and visit.

★ ★ ★ ★ ★ "A five-star neighbourhood theatre" Independent

As a registered charity [number 1137223] with no public subsidy, we rely on the kind support of our donors and volunteers. To find out how you can get involved visit parktheatre.co.uk.

## DEDICATION AND ACKNOWLEDGEMENTS

Charities on board: UnCut/Voices, Council of Ex-Muslims, The Vavengers, Safe Hands For Girls, 28 Too Many, National FGM Centre, La Fraternité Guinéenne, Forward, Global Media Campaign to End FGM, The Royal College of Midwives, Global Comfort.

Gloria Williams' and Lara Genovese's family and friends, Park theatre team, Sunday Surgery Scripts, Activist, Midwives, Actresses, Volunteers, Survivors and the cast and crew who have dedicated time to make the production possible.

UnCut/Voices

# CHARACTERS

CLEO – African British Female, playing age 25–30. Outspoken and feisty young woman who is a survivor of type 3 Female Genital Mutilation. She challenges the traditions and the community by sharing her trauma and her understanding of the social norms.

EVE - African British, playing age 38–43. A survivor of Female Genital Mutilation, she is a nurturing care giver who sits on the fence in regards to the FGM practise. She uses her submission to the culture and her 'mother-like' influence on Cleo to compensate for her sexual frustration and confusion.

WINNIE – African Female, playing age 50–70. Sierra Leone accent. An outspoken traditionalist and God-fearing older woman who is a survivor of Female Genital Mutilation. She uses her maturity and experience to influence and enforce younger women to embrace female circumcision.

# SETTING

London.
A house in present day.

# THE CUTTING
by Anni Domingo

She always knew that her day would come.
Girls are born for this, there is no option,
there is no choice, no right to complain,
no one wants to hear that it is wrong.
Her mother and grandmother survived,
she would too. It is compulsory, so they say.

The women must cut her up, snip at the bud
shave, carve, level it out, infibulate
that devil's tongue between her legs,
to give her a stainless, sinless body.
She too carries this burden of femininity,
her destiny of pain, so they say.

The women talk in low voices, ready for the task.
Cold breeze blows and sends warning signs.
Stripped naked, stretched apart, each limb
firmly held, by them, the holders of torso,
legs and arm, she is obedient and silent.
Her scream must be stitched in, so they say.

Pain eats into her flesh, it comes in waves
each worse than the one before, an ocean
of awareness, lost in a world of agony.
Unconscious, she cannot scream stop.
The lips sewn up leave only a little opening,
to answer the call of nature, so they say.
Herb paste soothe where vaginal lips had been.
Legs tied together with ropes from thighs to toes,
no moving, no writhing, she waits to heal.
Seal up that place, learn to sit, to stand,
do not bend or move those legs apart.
Practice the mermaid walk, so they say.

Now she's conscious of her marriage plight to come,
painful breaking through to create a passage again,
aware of birth dilemmas waiting to ambush her,
doubling the chances she might die, knows bitter
tears will flow at every stage for the rest of her life.
But she is clean and purified now, or so they say.

When will it stop, this perpetual hurt and abuse
of girls left with scars that will never heal?
We and our pain must ever grow up together
while we blindly seek something to separate us.
Without organs intact this is not a celebration,
this is our agonising eternal  punishment. So she says.

# ACT I

## Scene One

*It is mid-morning.* CLEO *has been staying in the room for three days,* EVE *enters the bedroom singing.*

EVE   PRINCESS GBEOFIA, PRINCESS GBEOFIA, THE STORY OF THE PREGNANT VIRGIN, QUEEN OF BEAUTY, QUEEN OF BEAUTY. THE MOST BEAUTIFUL GIRL IN THE WHOLE VILLAGE, WAITING, WANTING TO FIND HER PRINCE, A CREATURE COMES TO THE PALACE HOPING FOR HER HAND IN MARRIAGE, HE COMES WITH HER FAVOURITE FOOD,

PRINCESS GBEOFIA! PRINCESS GBEOFIA!

THE STORY OF THE PREGNANT VIRGIN, QUEEN OF BEAUTY.

*Lights up.* EVE *is sewing a red silk gown whilst* CLEO *lays on the bed next to a doll.*

Wake up Sleepin' Beauty. Dat's what I tell my husband to call me, Sleepin' Beauty. Me tell him I feel like a born again virgin and I'll die a virgin. He try tellin' me not to share my body wiv nobody – not even a wet finger, and den he himself don't even spill a single drop – I keep talkin' and he don't talk back. I say 'Oh don't worry 'bout me, I'm as tight as a gate, 'cos I wanna enter Heaven one day.' My clart is gettin' older and the heart between my legs too, you knaw... one side is larger dan the other coz it's stretchin', can you believe dat Cleo? The stitch is stretchin' ...Before I could close my legz and you couldn't see nothin'. Now one side of the stitch peeks thru like it don't wanna be no secret no more – like it ain't forbidden... So...what about a bath Cleo?

*Beat.*

You wanna have a bath babe?

CLEO *(no answer)*

EVE  I love to take a bath...but I hate it at the same time... It's like you get thirsty for water, but you reakin' of blood. Women bleed to love. You tek a shower and when the water hits you – you feel spat on...dontcha? ...Clee?

CLEO *(no answer)*

EVE  Yeh babe...sure. You need a bath babe. Let me know if you're onnit later yeh? But...but...don't think for a sec dat my blood isn't as hot or as red yours...

*Pause.*

CLEO *sleeps.* EVE *continues singing to herself whilst moving to the kitchen area.*

*Singing.*

GENTLE WOMAN, QUIET LIGHT, MORNING STAR SO STRONG AND BRIGHT, GENTLE MOTHER, PEACEFUL DOVE. TEACH US WISDOM, TEACH US LOVE.

EVE *continues humming the tune of the song.* WINNIE *enters.*

WINNIE  Thanks for doing that plate by the way.

EVE  Oh I'm not doing a big plate of food this time. I got some eggs and some toast, coz she's not eating nothing you or I cook.

WINNIE  She'll eat, coz you make some excellent eggs.

EVE  I don't know about that. *(Beat)* She needs to smell my kitchen when I'm mekin some of my potato leaf stew and my pepper chicken...oh yeh, she'll yam up my food. Hey Aunt Winnie you know some places they throw away a potato leaf thinkin' its dirty.

WINNIE  I know! And to think we cook it to perfection. I'll never forget the day my old Jamaican colleague said she saw Akees in the vegetable market smashed on the ground on her trip to Lagos. Stepped on, uncared. Made her want to start her own cookery business.

EVE  Too right. I love givin' some dirty potato leaves a makeover, get the palm oil right and you got your yummy stew. *(Beat)* She *is* beautiful, lookin' so peaceful laying with her dolly. Since she was brought here from her husband's, the only thing she mutters about is sum crap from those leaflets she reads.

WINNIE  That's what the clinics has been hypnotising her with. Please.

EVE  It's the feeling she wants.

WINNIE  So you actually got her talking?

EVE  Kinda. It's like living with a sound that don't make sense.

WINNIE  Just like that dog next door.

EVE  The labrador? I swear that dog has funny little ways of telling you something's wrong.

WINNIE  What's wrong is it's still running free.

EVE  I swear it barks so much it makes me wanna hold it in my arms and give it life. I loved a dog as a child, used to tell all my troubles to it.

WINNIE  That dog needs to be neutered, keep it docile, stop it from running wild. That's what's wrong with the world.

EVE  Did Kareem call?

WINNIE  No your husband did not call.

EVE  *OK.* Probably couldn't get service from Freetown. *(Beat)* I'm just done. He don't like no dress I sew for him. By the time he decides to lay me down, I'll be in the cemetery.

WINNIE  Do not be negative. A man enjoys a narrow passage. Your husband's a grown-up man who still needs to drip. So there's hope.

**EVE**  Even sum red scraps I stitch together. Every stitch I sew is like a kiss from me.

**WINNIE**  Well keep on stitching till you get that kiss.

**EVE**  You mean for me to wait? Us chicks wait our whole lives, for breasts, for proposals...

**WINNIE**  Oh just stop that talk.

**EVE**  Aunt Winnie it's true. My man don't chat or talk to me unless he's prayin'. I be cussin' – I be screamin' for him to hold me and he still don't even talk.

**CLEO** *is crying from the bed.*

*Silence.*

**EVE** *and* **WINNIE** *act busy, ignoring her cries. This happens for a few moments.*

I better go check on her.

**WINNIE**  Relax. Don't be so quick to jump when she moans. She's not moaning for you.

**EVE**  She could have had another nightmare.

*A moment later.* **EVE** *and* **WINNIE** *keep themselves busy and ignore* **CLEO**. **CLEO** *gives a few more cries, whilst* **EVE** *looks painfully uncomfortable.*

I better give Cleo her eggs.

**EVE** *attends to the plate of food.*

**WINNIE**  Be careful fixing that broken girl. You might get yourself cut.

**EVE** *exits with the plate of food.* **EVE** *goes to* **CLEO**'s *bed and sits the food down for* **CLEO** *who is half awake.* **EVE** *tries to get* **CLEO** *to take the food.* **CLEO** *knocks the tray of eggs offered by* **EVE** *on the floor.*

EVE *(cleaning up the food)* Naw. Naw. Naw babes. I'm not onnit. You know I don't like bendin' down when I be on my knees cleanin' up dis crap. Note dat, yeh? You gotta put something in your belly. I can't be cleanin' up dese eggs. You'll starve, get skinny and lose dose child givin' hips. *(Whilst still cleaning eggs)* It's da egg that has the choice, not the seed... The seed invades anything and gets pissed off tryna find the egg. You ain't like my husband...he likes his eggs mixed wiv flour...ain't dat weird? It would mek me fill so full in my belly – so tight – like I'm filled with sum big old life... Dat's one ting dat stands between me and my husband

*Pause.*

Now Cleo, you can chat or not chat. You could be here for a lifetime if you want, in dis dump. How you gonna stomach that? You gimme a chance and I could cook you your favourite food. You like potato leaf? I could play your favourite music and we can could do a lil dance?

CLEO *(no answer)*

EVE Or we could have a lil drink and talk about your favourite thingz in this world, you like that?

CLEO *(no answer)*

EVE Cleo, I need to know your favourite thingz and what you love... Can I tell you about my favourite thingz?

CLEO *(no answer)*

EVE Okay...well... I love to talk about new recipes, making clothes and beauty. Could even do your make-up and nails, could even do your hair. I love painting nails and I love making naturally beautiful girls look even more beautiful...once goin' to the London zoo as a child a peacock showed me its feathers...never seen so many colours on one creature in my life... It had so many colours and shapes, standin' proud... tall...strong. I knew then I loved natural beauty... So, Miss Cleo...can I pretty-up your pretty face to kill time?

**CLEO** *does not answer.*

Now don't go blamin' your misery on these lil stitches, it ain't their fault...the seed of the relationship need to be nurtured, naturally.

**CLEO** *continues to ignore her.*

So juss take it den, tek his piece like a man, like you never were a chick – like you never had a third dick yourself – like you never hadda hole...just tek the damn dick.

*Pause.*

Do you want eggs or apples or what?

## Scene Two

*Later that day* EVE *enters the bedroom attempting to talk to* CLEO *again.*

EVE   Wat's up Clee Clee. Watcha think? Watcha think? You think I'll look cute? *(Showing* CLEO *the red garment)* Girl you gotta let me fix dat hair so we can both be cute together and dance... I was thinkin' how much I have been missin' my dancing... You know I juss love to dance?

CLEO   *(no answer)*

EVE   Now I know *you* can dance, I bet you went clubbin' at uni right? You gotta love da drums – I know I can dance to any drum... You love the drums in Sierra Leone, right babe?

WINNIE *enters the bedroom with the tray of food.*

WINNIE   I got you sum fresh eggs *again*, so sit up and get sum protein.

EVE   I was tellin' Clee about my dancing. Um, you knaw, juss, juss comfortin' her from those nightmares.

WINNIE   Nightmares? All this talk of nightmares! Forget all that and you've gotta get your strength back for your husband.

CLEO   *(pause)* Why? What am I supposed to do with it?

WINNIE   So the mute is talking now.

CLEO   Yeh *I'm* talking.

WINNIE   Don't talk too much—

CLEO   *I'm talking.*

WINNIE   You juss stop *that* kinda talk.

CLEO   Stop what kinda talk? No one gives a flying frigid fuck what I think or feel but I need to stop talking. How you do it?

WINNIE   Do what?

CLEO   Believe in dese dumb-ass laws made up by dumb people?

WINNIE  From what I see the people you been hanging with don't seem any better.

CLEO  Oh you mean my husband? He juss always needs a tight fist in me, thass all.

WINNIE  I'm talking 'bout them people in that clinic tryna convince you to hate your body and allow 'em to fix it like they're your 'saviours'.

*To* EVE.

I cannot believe we live in a world where any girl can go sneaking off to a midwife as though she's been possessed like sum whore.

*To* EVE.

Do these young girlz want men this bad?

EVE  *(curious)* So all these years of giving birth, you never thought about it?

WINNIE  No I haven't. Why would I?

EVE  *(no answer)*

WINNIE  Why would I?

EVE  The problems at childbirth. The baby getting stuck, the complications. Aunt Winnie you've had dis more than—

WINNIE  Don't you dare. I'm here coz of the blood of people who fought wars to protect us. I know that the stitches, the sewing, the cutting, it is not, it is not beautiful, it isn't ugly, it isn't sexy, it is just a stitch. And you are not broken Cleo.

CLEO  *Yes I am.*

WINNIE  Cleo. If we let you have that reversal, that meks you an open target. Sweetie the stitch is for your protection, we tryna save you.

CLEO  What do you mean save me?

WINNIE  From rape, diseases… I know the pain of a partner you love is hard to take sometimes…

**CLEO**  Who are you lot? I wanna be cut open!

**WINNIE**  Cleo.

**CLEO**  I *need* to be cut open!

**WINNIE**  Look Cleo –

**CLEO**  What do you lot want from me?

**WINNIE**  Accept the sewing of fertility and keep your role with God.

**CLEO**  *You know* I don't believe in God Aunt Winnie.

**WINNIE**  Ain't possible for you not to believe.

**CLEO**  What? I'm not onnit.

**WINNIE**  A white man you want? Is that it?

**CLEO**  It's stitches, it's stitches.

**WINNIE**  It's deeper than you, deeper than those needles – deeper than blood. It's preservin' your womb for the life that grows in you— You gonna eat dem eggs or what?

**CLEO**  What about feeling my own senses? My life?

**WINNIE**  You juss don't know about life. God loves you in the pain – like prickin' your finger on a thorn – he loves all dem feelings in you. I know you got lost somewhere and your daddy wanted you to stay with me.

**CLEO**  I don't wanna be here like some dead animal. I need to get back what my daddy stole from me. My daddy lied on me that it was time to get my gift. I loved him coz he knew what I needed. I was the seed of his... I got dat gift – dat fucked up flesh knifed off *my* life.

**WINNIE**  It *was* a gift Cleo. A gift.

**CLEO**  A gift? It was a curse! The bitches—

**EVE**  Alright. She needs to sleep.

**WINNIE**  Naw it ain't alright, she can't talk to me like this.

**EVE**  She's tired.

**WINNIE**  She's rude.

*Beat.*

Now you better eat those eggs, let it marinate in your body, give you some strength.

**CLEO**  Nooo, *please.*

**WINNIE** *exits and* **EVE** *stays.*

Please just go away.

**EVE**  You're the special one babes and he opened you up better than my man did. Believe that.

**EVE** *exits and leaves* **CLEO** *alone.*

*Lights gone.*

## Scene Three

*It is evening.* WINNIE *is talking to* CLEO *who is in bed.*
EVE *is also present in the room.*

WINNIE  We Africans all come from a place where...where you
could be walking juss walking on a land above diamonds...
bet, the closest thing to a diamond rock you girlz have seen...
probably at a jewellery store. Oh no but up country in Sierra
Leone, you could be playing near a river and start digging
the soil with a stick and pick up a heavy clump of dirt...
keep on scraping and scraping and scraping and scraping...
then...a piece of treasure is in your hand... Diamonds in the
rough should be hard to touch—

EVE  That's right Clee, when you become a diamond you'll see
why life had to pressure you Cleo. You don't need an incision.

CLEO  *(no answer)*

WINNIE  Dat's how us women need to be Cleo. We here to mek
sure your wings are clipped dat way. You hearin' me Clee?
*(Pause)* The needle helps the hole. God cut down dat hole
coz it looked too *masculine*.

CLEO  You don't know...you juss don't know, he meks me bleed...

WINNIE  Da blood of all girlz is sacred Cleo. In our culture
the blood of chiefs is smeared on faces you know, like a
re-birth of the spirit – that's beautiful – to have the blood
of an Angel on her husband's blooded weapon.

CLEO  Please...juss stop chattin'.

WINNIE  The extra flesh it's not needed.

CLEO  *(she begins to cry)* Please...

WINNIE  *(to EVE)* Oh, I know what's been said out there, you
think I don't? They are trying to have you girlz cut back
open before getting pregnant now. The news talks like we're
mutilated animals, like sum research project.

EVE  Aunt Winnie?

**WINNIE**  What did I say?

**EVE**  Please, she's tired.

**WINNIE**  I'll come back later.

**EVE**  *(to* **WINNIE***)* She's stressed, you know?

**WINNIE**  ...Right. I'm sure. I'm gonna call my daughters.

**WINNIE** *exits.*

**EVE**  You don't need to tell me nothing. With me here, you ain't gotta answer to nothin'. I ain't judgin'. I'm here when you need someone to talk to 'bout the pain you feel. Just sitting here whenever your shell is ready to crack...

*Pause.*

**EVE** *gets up to go and get some apples. She holds one out to* **CLEO***.* **CLEO** *looks.* **EVE** *places an apple on the bed.* **CLEO** *stares for a while and begins to eat it.* **EVE** *watches* **CLEO** *for a while and then begins to go deep in thought. A moment lingers of* **CLEO** *still eating and* **EVE** *just thinking and watching.*

It's like, it's like – I never blackout when I think 'bout my Bondo ceremony. People be tweetin' sayin' 'it's trauma', 'it's a crime', 'we need help'. But naw – how can it be when I just love to remember the sound of them drums – you remember your drums? Dem, dem drum beats dat let the whole bush know dat you a woman. That's why I think I love to dance...them drums beatin' in my heart, got every woman in the forest dancing and cheering for me. Aww dem sweet old ladies...washing my parts after the cuttin' by the river, so I knew I wasn't *dirty*. So like I said, I like to dance... I like to stare at a river... You know when I used to work in Regent's Park, I'd walk from Camden and don't laugh but I be juss standin' by a river, I might even get a lil tingle sometimes... So embarrassin' when I was twelve I used to go bike riding in the park on Saturdays, I would sit by the water and randomly start laughin'. I'd be just sittin' there lookin' at my reflection...

CLEO *(a moment)* And? What you never wanted to jump in?

EVE I'll juss pretend you never just said that.

CLEO But I did though.

*Pause.*

But I did though.

EVE *(pause)*

CLEO ...I done told my daddy, my uncle played footsie with da 'dirty' 'tween my legs... He den sent me to Freetown to get it chopped off... I was *seven.*

EVE That's his fault? You got your party afterwards did you not?

CLEO Aww, I did. My ceremony was so sweet. They took me to a beautiful place... I got told da ceremony was for female leaders, yeh fuckin' right. Dem women blindfolded me, told me to open my mouth for sweet food... I thought, this is a fun way to grow up— They stuffed my mouth with cloth, so I couldn't scream... How sweet. I stopped praying that night. They gave me this dolly and I picked up a needle and wished my uncle would die in the war. And he did. I wanted to protect other girlz. That's da power that a dream and a needle should make.

EVE Wow. Dat's not what I meant. I'm sorry you feel dat way Clee.

CLEO Yeh, I ain't prayin'.

EVE You're not praying?

CLEO God ain't listening. Why pray when da Higher Being and my tight-knit, tight-stitched, bitched-up family sold me off like cloth.

EVE I'm... I'm... I'm truly sorry Clee.

CLEO Naw you ain't.

EVE I *am* sorry. They were juss giving you a sacred gift of being a wife.

CLEO  A gift? Damaged.

EVE  Clee.

CLEO  *Fuck* dem.

EVE  Your bloods is thicker.

CLEO  There's a hurtin' hole where love used to be. Dat hole in me now sends burnin' fire and water up my blood.

EVE  ...What done mek you soo special Clee? What meks you so special? I say you gotta gift, you say you're fucked. Tell me Cleo, am I fucked too?

*Pause.*

Am I doh? I stick to the law that says we become honorable wives.

CLEO  Why Eve?

EVE  To make you honourable like all of us.

CLEO  All women are unique.

EVE  And you think you're better? Your feelins ain't real sis. Your husband, *Akmid*, his reality is what's real.

CLEO  I never chose to be married to that rapist.

EVE  Stop saying that word. It's our law.

CLEO  Whose law?

EVE  ...

CLEO  Naw, naw, naw dey ain't real. I took all my feelings and Akmid's 'n' buried dem inside me. With him rippin' thru to me – me holdin' him tight in our room. I knew I was tryna kill him and he knew it too. I pulled his prick hard and he hung *nowhere* for dat moment. You ever heard dat silence, hearin' da bloodstream move? Naw you ain't, have ya? When the air don't move, the stars, da Earth and whatever shit holds it altogether. Now I'm here and you lot think I'm sum witch... He don't care 'bout my sanctified, fucked-up flesh. Ain't got no interest in da Higher Bein' yeh. His place ain't here yeh. With your holier than thou eggs. I ain't eatin nothing you've cooked. Juss, juss saggy looking. What *have* you...what have you...what have you got?

EVE Play da game sis. Juss stop chattin' back to Aunt Winnie, ain't worth the fight nor the pain – juss say nothin. I know you wanna go back to da body you were born with... sometimes...even I do.

## Scene Four

*Later that evening in the kitchen,* WINNIE *is sitting very still in the dark drinking tea.* CLEO *wanders in as she is looking for something and at first cannot see* WINNIE.

WINNIE  Do you know how strange it is to be a woman who sleeps with a doll.

*Chuckles awkwardly.* CLEO *is startled and notices* WINNIE.

Hello Cleo.

CLEO  Hi. I mean, good evening Aunt Winnie.

WINNIE  Come and sit with me please.

> CLEO *is hesitant, then goes to sit down.*

So you're well fed, yes?

CLEO  Yeh.

WINNIE  Comfortable enough?

CLEO  *(nods head)* Um... It's all good thanks.

WINNIE  Sure?

CLEO  It's perfect.

WINNIE  Good.

> *Pause.*

You want to know how the magic all works?

CLEO  How what works?

> WINNIE *brings out* CLEO*'s doll from behind her back and dangles it in front of her.* CLEO *passively attempts to get her doll back.*

So you juss gonna show me a thirty-year-old's doll in front of me? I was lookin for that.

**WINNIE** This thing looks so old it's like – it's like one of the seven wonders.

**CLEO** I've had it since I was a kid.

**WINNIE** Yes. It looks familiar.

*Beat.*

Cleo, I owe you an apology.

*Pause.*

How naughty of me to touch your dolly without me asking you.

**CLEO** Naw it's okay, juss wondered where Happiness was.

**WINNIE** 'Happiness'?

**CLEO** My doll.

**WINNIE** Oh – let me explain my dear. I lifted your doll when you were in the toilet and I was fluffing your pillow. I just picked it up and took it with me without thinking.

**CLEO** Yeh nah it's—

**WINNIE** Rather than put it back while you're sleeping, I just kept it with me. How naughty of me.

**CLEO** Aunt Winnie, I'm a big thirty-year-old wiv a doll, it ain't a big deal – I juss get nervous without it, it's juss—

**CLEO** *finally manages to grab her doll back.*

**WINNIE** Immature... Well I'll let you know, I can handle any doll.

*Beat.*

That's what I remember being so special about the Bondo celebration, me and all the women in that bush knew you and the other girls had a heightened gift of nurture, strength and power. There were passages, pregnancies...marriages... births and deaths too.

**CLEO** Right.

**WINNIE**   So, what about your uncle Martin? Where were you when your family heard that news.

**CLEO**   Who?

**WINNIE**   Your Uncle Martin who rested with God that summer.

*Pause.*

Where were you and that doll?

**CLEO**   Where was I?

**WINNIE**   Where were you and that doll when he died?

**CLEO**   I don't wanna think about that...Probably playing by the river wiv sum village kids or somethin'.

**WINNIE**   How old were you again?

**CLEO**   You know how old I waz. I was *seven*.

**WINNIE**   *Right.* Yes you were the youngest and the most beautiful, special, strong, courageous and powerful seven year old the bush had ever ever seen. Tell me more Cleo.

*Pause.*

Look at me sweetie. So, where was your father?

**CLEO**   I donno, at work or sumthin'.

**WINNIE**   The Queen of the Bush is playing with her little doll... her father is at work... *(Beat)* Well...your Uncle is up there now.

**CLEO**   Yes – I'm sure he's restin' somewhere.

*Pause.*

**WINNIE**   You know where I was when your mother was carrying you? I was a mother of two praying for my third child... When you were born...found out I was pregnant with my son. *(Pause)* Sometimes you know when a Queen is born...you know how? ...Miracles happen when she arrives... Oh Cleo, the more powerful you become the more you can withstand pressure and sacrifice – you don't think I have yearned for needs in my body that I cannot have?

CLEO  Right.

WINNIE  Everyone needs to be you Cleo… Every woman in that bush – that summer wanted to be like you… We all felt your blessing, your beauty, your strength. I want to celebrate your strength. I want to celebrate your strength again just like that summer. Let me and the community protect you – not the clinics.

*Pause.*

Now Cleo… We are keeping those stitches.

WINNIE *exits and leaves* CLEO *alone to think for a while.*

## Scene Five

*It is the next day.* **WINNIE** *and* **EVE** *are in the kitchen.*
**WINNIE** *performs a spiritual libation by laying drops*
*of drink on the kitchen floor. There is music playing in*
*the background. There are also some cocktail ingredients*
*on the table.* **EVE** *has picked a flower.* **CLEO** *enters.*

**EVE**  Got a flower for you Cleo – wasn't sure what your favourite
flower was, and I couldn't decide on tulips or pink roses, so
I picked these from the blossom tree, hope the neighbours
don't get mad.

**WINNIE**  They better not, they runnin' around with two horny
dogs that keep barking and making my blood pressure jump.

**CLEO**  *(pause)*

**EVE**  Let's forget about some dogs and celebrate a real woman
today.

**WINNIE**  We are very proud of you Cleo.

> **EVE** *comforts* **CLEO.**

**EVE**  Very proud of you baby.

> *Beat.*

**WINNIE**  I only drink when there's a celebration.

**EVE**  What would my Kareem say if he saw me drinking.

**WINNIE**  You taken care of Aunt Winnie coz her daughters don't
care to phone everyday... Now it's your turn, plus my drinks
are sweet fruit punch. It's like drinking juice but feelin' all
saucy, but you don't know why.

**EVE**  Okay Aunt Winnie, please.

**WINNIE**  It's juss a cup of sugar, sum mango juice, some coconut
juice, some cut apples and a little bit of vodka. *Relax.* Your
husband might actually like you for it. And he'll be the one
serving you breakfast in the mornings.

**AUNT WINNIE** *gives a chuckle.*

**EVE**  Get out of here. I like my meat well done.

**WINNIE**  OOOH! Miss also likes her coffee black. Oh and she can dance the day away.

**CLEO** *begins to go in deep thought.*

**EVE**  Yes I sure can. And I do hair.

*To* **CLEO.**

You want me to do your hair babe?

**CLEO**  ...

**EVE**  Can do your nails too. Anything to pretty-up that arm.

(**WINNIE** *takes off her necklace and bracelet from herself and adorns* **CLEO.** **EVE** *goes to collect her beauty bag.)*

**EVE**  Cleo – what on Earth did you do to your arm?

**CLEO** *hides her arm, which looks like it has been bruised, and continuously looks deep in thought.*

**CLEO**  Nothin'.

**EVE**  Looks like you been digging in there a bit.

**CLEO**  ...

**WINNIE**  She's fine. This is soo exciting. It's like I'm present at a ceremony. There's something so wonderful when a woman chooses to stay a woman.

**CLEO** *goes into deep thought.*

Miss Eve, I chose for you too.

**EVE**  You chose what?

**WINNIE** *gestures as if to say 'One minute', she dances over to a bag and slowly brings out a piece of clothing and lifts it out.*

**WINNIE**  To Eve.

WINNIE *laughs, as she presents a red vulgar lingerie outfit.*

EVE  Aunt Winnie! You know that this ain't me.

WINNIE  I'm sorry, forgive me. I juss thought you needed a bit of inspiration – buy yourself more lace sweetie.

EVE  That's mean.

WINNIE  *(laughing)* Eve, I love you more than my granny panties!

EVE  I *love* sewing my own things.

WINNIE  Love sewing? That red shimmy. Is it a gift for you or your husband?

CLEO*'s deep thought begins to manifest in her posture.*

EVE  Both.

WINNIE  You *do* gift him don't you?

EVE  Well when he's being sweet and I don't feel like hitting him with a frying pan.

WINNIE  Okay, okay – I have made my mango fruit punch.

*She brings them all a glass.*

Cleo is a woman. She's a Queen.

*Beat.*

EVE *looks at* CLEO *with concern.*

*Beat.*

Cleo the woman. To *all* women like us.

WINNIE *and* EVE *raise their drinks and take a gulp.*

CLEO *is shaking.*

EVE  *(sadly watching* CLEO*)* Sweet. Real sweet.

WINNIE  Could have been sweeter if I had more apples but Miss Cleo over here has eaten up all my apples, it's okay Cleo. Cleo?

EVE *notices* CLEO's *frenzy and immediately snaps out of her drowsy state and quickly reacts.*

EVE  Oh Lord Cleo!

WINNIE  What's wrong with her. Cleo!

EVE *and* WINNIE *rush towards her and hold her to keep her still whilst* CLEO *has a panic attack.*

EVE  She needs some water.

CLEO  *(struggling)* No.

WINNIE  Yes Cleo. Do not argue.

EVE *tries to get water.*

EVE  Should I call the doctor?

WINNIE  No! She just needs to drink.

EVE  But we don't know what's wrong with her.

CLEO *struggling to talk.*

CLEO  Don't...talk about me...like I ain't here.

EVE *comes with the water.*

EVE  You just need more water!

*She forces the water down* CLEO's *throat.* CLEO *begins to calm down gasping for breath.*

You gotta take sum water and not be so stubborn.

CLEO  Oh man.

*Pause.*

EVE *comforts* CLEO.

I am what you lot wanted! I was juss a kid. I can't do dis no more. I need a proper counsellor... Sorry Aunt Winnie but I need to talk to someone...

WINNIE  What? To talk to who? And about what and who?

*Pause.*

Please don't play a hard rock when you really are a gem... I find that a broken girl becomes a beautiful woman and can change da world... We are supposed to be celebrating womanhood, ladies. No one gets upset during celebration time. Aunt Winnie's house rules. We could really do with Eve's dancing to some big loud drums rights now.

EVE *comforts* CLEO *like a mother talking to young child.*

EVE  How about we sit and we chill and we relax and I can do your hair, real, *real* nice. You like dat babe?

*Pause.*

Cleo – come now and let's do your hair, babe.

EVE *takes* CLEO *to her room while* WINNIE *is drinking her punch, getting drunk.*

*Lights out.*

## Scene Six

*Later that day.* CLEO *is in the bedroom talking to* EVE, *who is outside of the bedroom. At first we can hear her but we can only see* CLEO.

CLEO  Come on Eve! Does it take that long to get in a shimmy!

EVE  *(in the kitchen)* I'm comin'! Juss need to get the fit right!

*We can see that* CLEO *is in some sort of emotional pain but is trying to fight it.*

CLEO  Is this a trick just to get me to talk?! We gonna do these nails or what?

*CLEO walks into the kitchen and sees EVE wearing the red shimmy she has been sewing, she has a glass of water.*

*Pause.*

CLEO  You look nice.

EVE  Really?

CLEO  Beautiful.

*Pause.*

*EVE goes to get a cup of tea and hands to CLEO.*

EVE  Drink this please.

CLEO  Naw. I'm alright.

EVE  Let this do the work and not your hard head.

CLEO  I don't need it.

EVE  But you start thinking too much and...

CLEO  Alright—

EVE  And you start hearing...

CLEO  *Alright.*

EVE   Cleo I'm on your side, but when you get overwhelmed, you get sad and we don't know what you'll do... Please.

CLEO *hesitantly drinks the tea.* EVE *begins to collect nail polish and starts painting* CLEO*'s nails.*

EVE   You know... I thought if I tried to give my husband what he needed, he'd give me what I needed.

CLEO   He don't force you does he—

EVE   No. He don't do nothing... He don't touch me coz I'm sewn just like you.

*Pause.*

CLEO   But does he—

EVE   He's gentle, sometimes. He was treated for bruises trying.

CLEO   ...

EVE   After three months tryin', he never penetrated again.

CLEO   Never?

EVE   Not even an inch of him. Each time he touched I bled. But Cleo it don't mean he was thinking of rape. Watchin' him lay wounded and wet wiv his own tears – him waking up holding his piece – lookin' like it don't belong to him. What can I do?

CLEO   You still a virgin Eve?

EVE   I don't know.

CLEO   If you don't know how good it's suppose to feel, den you still a virgin.

EVE   And what about you?

CLEO   I... I guess I am one too. But he's your husband! He's a fool to not give you what you need.

EVE   He's gentle and he's a friend. A friendship of sadness. I married him coz he was kind.

*(pause)* What would you do?

CLEO  He's such a coward to not take you to get help.

EVE  He's not a coward, he's been hurt like a child. And I see dat I love him like a child, since I can't have my own child. But I'm staying coz hope is always possible.

CLEO  Oh please, whatever. I'm hoping you're prepared when he smashes someone else.

EVE *pauses and looks in shock.*

Naw I'm not saying he will doh.

EVE  Yeh he does.

CLEO  Nah he don't.

EVE  He can't love me if his veins don't pump through me.

CLEO  How can he not wanna create a child with you?

EVE  He can't stand the pain.

CLEO  Yours or his?

EVE  Both – he can't stand the blood.

CLEO  Okay. Yours or his?

EVE  Mine. But birth is such a beautiful thing. I'm sure the feeling would be better than sex.

CLEO  F– that chat Eve. Betcha give him a gun and send him to war and he'll be brave to see that blood. What do *you* really want?

EVE  *Me?*

*Pause.*

I dunno... I want...a house...two beautiful children...

CLEO  Great Eve, juss great! How da stork gonna drop da egg if the only shiver you getting is his cold shoulder?

EVE  I don't look like you Cleo. I know how I look and what you think.

*Beat.*

You think that I'm weak and saggy lookin'?

CLEO  Oh Eve I was juss pissed at you for not listening to me. But I think *you're* beautiful.

EVE  Really? Thank you Cleo.

CLEO  I do. I think you're beautiful. You're like a teacher.

*Pause.*

EVE  And you are nuts.

CLEO  You wanna see something?

CLEO *shows* EVE *her hands.*

My secret. Look at that.

EVE  What am I looking at? A bump?

CLEO  People say it's like an extra finger or whatever. I've alwayz loved it. Scares off the men.

EVE  You are nuts Cleo. It juss looks like a bump. It's not so bad. I'm stuck with who I am.

CLEO  You're a good woman Eve. You're a giver and you're kind. A life with you would be a life of love.

*A moment.*

You gotta make love to make life... I guess.

*Pause.*

CLEO *leans forward and kisses* EVE *on the forehead. A moment of locking eyes.* CLEO *turns* EVE*'s head towards hers.*

*A silhouette of* WINNIE *is by the doorway.*

**End of Act I**

# ACT II

## Scene Seven

*Later the same day.* CLEO *is sitting on a chair and*
EVE *is standing behind the chair in a 'hair stylist and
client' image.*

EVE  Now Clee, this is the dumbest thing you gonna do – juss
coz you upset don't mean you gotta change your look.

CLEO  Luv you Eve, but I ain't gonna debate this shit wiv you.
I'm not here for a lecture.

EVE  I'm not cutting your hair!

CLEO  What's the big deal?

EVE  Damn Clee! All three of us have been cut the same. You're
as beautiful as you are.

CLEO  Okay fine, I'll cut it myself!

*Pause.*

I will.

EVE *reaches for the scissors and attempts but is distracted
and continues to talk.*

EVE  Cleo. What you sayin'? What you sayin'?

*Pause.*

You just gonna sit like dis? *(Beat)* I mean I liked the fact
that you a girly-girl and pay real cute attention to yourself,
'cept what you did to your arm, now you got me razoring
this hair too.

CLEO  Stop talkin' about my arm.

EVE *once again attempts and then continues to speak.*

EVE  You think some man's gonna look at you and not want
you in his bed? Even if you tried to ugly yourself? So now
you wanna be ugly? Ugly arms, short hair...manz woulda
already looked at your legs, your arms, your batty and your
titties too, what does it matter about having short hair. Why?

CLEO  I don't want no one touching me anymore, that's *why.*
*Please,* juss cut my hair. Juss get it off me.

EVE  Okay fine, fine.

EVE *starts to cut the hair whilst* CLEO *looks distressed.*

EVE  Can use a razor too you knaw. Can't believe you.

*Pause.*

Chat to me.

CLEO *says nothing.*

Please chat to me Clee. Why?

CLEO  *(pause)* I don't wanna cover up anymore, not my face
not my mind, not my scars, nothin'.

EVE  But you survived the cuttin'.

CLEO  I survived it? Nah man survival's BS... I hate people sayin'
dat... I have to listen to sum chick at work talk about her
honeymoon, her wedding night, her love makin', with rose
petals and candles an' shit... I'm juss staring at her and I'm
like... I don't even know what she chattin' about...not one
mention of no painkillers she has to take after the sex. Or,
or, or like me havin my stomach churnin' the whole day of
my weddin'... *(Pause)* terrified when all the guests leave
coz I knew I was gonna get it dat night – I knew I was
gonna get it on my wedding day...first time I ever travelled
abroad, whilst I was goin back to Africa, my friends were
goin' Disney Land – they come back with a tan...and...and
I come back with...a gift.

*Pause.*

Don't even chat to me about that time of the month – sum girlz in my class used to say, 'juss go on the pill, it hurts less', I be thinkin' naw you don't get it. Sum chicks I know joke about goin' home to make love to their man and I'm thinkin' – I just about survived last night… I don't wannabe a survivor anymore. I juss want to live.

## Scene Eight

*Later that night,* WINNIE *is in the kitchen anxiously on her hands and knees cleaning a specific spot on the floor. The mango punch is on the floor while she scrubs. She stays focused and cleaning for a few moments.*

EVE *(offstage)* Aunt Winnie...?

*No answer.*

Aunt Winnie...?

EVE *enters.* WINNIE *is cleaning anxiously focused on the spot on the floor.*

WINNIE  I can't get this out.

EVE  Huh?

WINNIE  I said I just can't get this out.

EVE  ...

WINNIE  It's here. It's right *here* and you're all juss, juss walking all over it.

EVE  Walkin' on what?

WINNIE  My baby's blood. Like my baby boy is just some *animal.*

EVE  Aunt Winnie please go to sleep. It's too late for all this. Go to sleep and wake up in the morning.

EVE *moves closer.*

Please juss—

WINNIE  Child don't stand in that spot!

EVE  ...

WINNIE  I can... I can get up each day, feed myself, clothe myself, leave the house. I could even run through Primrose Hill if I wanted, but Gabriel can't. How will I ever know how wonderful he could have been? My baby boy. He would be a man by now...he would sit down at the gates and I would sing and Gabriel my baby would fall off to sleep and tell me to wake him up when it's time to open the gates.

EVE  *Oh man*, Aunt Winnie.

WINNIE  I was supposed to go first, not him.

EVE  That was long ago. Please don't talk that way. You will make yourself sick.

WINNIE  I was always ready to go first, not my baby. Ask Cleo if those midwives of hers could ever heal my soul.

EVE  This is too much—

AUNT WINNIE  You ask her if them clinics would ever bring my son back.

EVE  Aunt Winnie!

WINNIE  The closest thing she knows to a mother is holding that ugly doll. Same ugly doll we gave her in the Bondo, now she's holding it tightly in my home.

*Beat.*

I'm not a child abuser, Eve.

EVE  I know. We have nothing to be scared of.

WINNIE  I can just see it now, her in 'The Elizabeth Garret Ward' talking about all of us.

EVE  Stop being dramatic. Cleo's not doing anything. She's safe with me.

*Pause.*

WINNIE  You know God don't make mistakes Eve. He sees everything.

*Pause.*

You still like men Eve?

EVE  I'm married.

*Pause.*

Aunt Winnie please.

WINNIE  How do you not know she hasn't got *your* hairs in a bag.

EVE  *Please* – just stop—

WINNIE  Stop what Miss Eve?

EVE  Stop scaring me! Cleo's fine, she's not sum witch.

WINNIE  You just like her. Creeping around each other like a bunch of men – mekin' *me* out to be the witch. You're juss like her.

EVE  The world and da women are more important than a stitch!

*Beat.*

WINNIE  So all of a sudden you know her better, like you both stitched-up together!

EVE  And you too busy worrying about nothing!

WINNIE  Why you think you ain't got no babies? You all chopping her hair off. Cleo is turning into a man before our Goddamn eyes and you're sitting back letting it happen. Do you want a baby?

EVE  You know I need a baby.

WINNIE  Then it's her. Cleo's in your way.

EVE  Don't you blame her. Don't you do it.

WINNIE  She don't honour God like you do.

*EVE wells up.*

EVE  Oh my God! My God.

WINNIE  You're not a bad woman.

EVE  I am, I am.

*We can hear the sounds of CLEO beginning to cry from the bedroom.*

WINNIE  I'm trying to be a guardian to you girlz, I'm not a child abuser.

EVE  My God. I gotta get closer to you.

EVE *begins to chant a private prayer whilst* WINNIE *watches her.* CLEO *is laying and still crying in her sleep.*

CLEO  Eve!

EVE *is alerted to* CLEO*'s scream and immediately reacts to go and help her, then painfully resists and remains still.*

Eve! Eve! I need you! ...I... I... I need you!

CLEO *is spinning within a nightmare.*

Stop it! *Stop it! Arhhhgg! I ca...I can't...* Eve! Shh, shh, shh, please stop, please stop... Eve!

EVE *reacts to* CLEO*'s cry for help and can feel her movements trying to fight the pain.* EVE *is hurting because of her reluctance to help* CLEO.

EVE *exits.*

## Scene Nine

*It is the next morning.* CLEO *who now has short hair is in her room awake.* EVE *enters the room and is cleaning whilst singing.*

**EVE**
GENTLE WOMAN QUIET NIGHT, MORNING STAR SO STRONG AND BRIGHT. GENTLE WOMAN PEACEFUL DOVE, TEACH US WISDOM TEACH US LOVE.

**CLEO**  I... I was calling you.

**EVE**  *(abruptly)* I know I heard you.

**CLEO**  *(pause) I'm fucked.* I'm...I'm fucked for life.

*Struggling to speak.*

I can hear these sounds...and...and I hear...screaming and my weak hands...

**EVE**  I'm not your counsellor Cleo.

**CLEO**  I know (?)

*Pause.*

Please talk to me Eve.

**EVE**  Just picking up strands of your hair. I failed at keeping the floor clean.

**CLEO**  Fine I'll help you—

**EVE**  No.

**CLEO**  Look... I juss wanna thank you for your hand, that's all. It was really what I needed. You're a giving person Eve and you made me...

**EVE**  Made you what?

**CLEO**  *Feel.* Thank you—

**EVE**  ...I think it's time you started making plans to go back home.

**CLEO**  You want me to go?

EVE  We can't win. I can't win Cleo. If you just moved on, you would focus on your own life and let Akmid take care of you.

CLEO  ...Huh? If...if...if you're ashamed, or you wanna act the bitch—

EVE  It's unnatural.

*Pause.*

It's unnatural. I'm not like that. I don't *do* that. Maybe I...I'll talk to Aunt Winnie and let her know you're ready.

CLEO  If you care about me, you'll keep your mouth shut.

*Pause.*

coz I ain't groanin' for God, 'the man upstairs'. You all of a sudden ain't 'like that?'.

EVE  I give up. Let's give up. I'll tell Aunt Winnie I'm a bad influence on you.

EVE *starts to exit heading for the door.*

CLEO  I'll cut myself open.

*Pause.*

EVE *is silenced and startled by the comment and stops as she heads for the door.*

EVE  You wouldn't.

CLEO*'s exposes her cut arm to* EVE.

Would you?

*Pause.*

Don't know how you can break your family's heart like this.

CLEO  Don't have nothing to do with my family... If you'd been forced like I have. You'd see how little God cared about you and your frigid secret.

AUNT WINNIE *enters.* WINNIE *is looking hard at* CLEO*'s new short haircut.*

*Pause.*

WINNIE  So this is the hair, huh?

*Pause.*

You didn't even want sum braids, a weave, a wig...nothin'?

EVE  It's what she wanted Aunt Winnie.

WINNIE  OK... Not even dreadlocks?

EVE  Aunt Winnie, let it go.

WINNIE  Fine, fine – I mean ladies you're supposed to be pleasing your man's eye. It's all part of the union and it's for the children. Between me, an' God – I married one of the most worthless men on this planet – *but,* have the most beautiful daughters; although ungrateful, and I don't really like them sometimes, they are my treasures.

CLEO  It's my body, not just for my man and not for no children.

WINNIE  *(to* CLEO*)* Oh, is that from those silly FGM 'women saviours'? What do they have that women in our community don't?

CLEO  They are not silly women. They are *special* women. *Specialist* midwives, health advocates and they ain't cutters from the Bondo who scraped my clit with a knife and stitched me up leaving me with a tiny hole—

WINNIE  *I* didn't cut you! I think I know what your problem is... I heard you bought your mum pain in her conception of you, you couldn't even drink her breast milk.

CLEO  ...

WINNIE  They say, the baby that rejects her mother's breast milk will never be full. We want your belly to be round like the Earth – but first we need to keep that dark hole for the father to find...

CLEO  I need to see a counsellor. That's all I ask.

WINNIE  Why?

CLEO  They put a girl with a counsellor at the clinic. They chat to them about the different types and sexual experience.

WINNIE  A counsellor?

CLEO  Yes and a midwife too.

WINNIE  Why? Why do you want to do this?

CLEO  For my peace of mind. They can fix the problem with the construction of the narrowing. Can you believe that! They say it's a reversal Aunt Winnie. A reversal! You can pee naturally and *give birth naturally*! You can really really live!

WINNIE  *(pause)* That's what you believe is it?

*Pause.*

I see... *(Beat)* Nobody hears me. Our type have healthy babies all the time. It's misleading. What?! A 'reversal', *please*. It is not gold dust and it is not going to undo anything. These fake rumours about horror births. There's a separate God for children.

CLEO  You went into labour with Gabriel your son? Right Aunt Winnie? Your third pregnancy.

WINNIE  So?

CLEO  Wasn't he meant to be a year younger than me?

*Pause.*

You carried him for the full nine months and then what happened?

WINNIE  There were complications.

CLEO  Why?

WINNIE  What's with all these questions?

CLEO  Is that why you named him Gabriel?

WINNIE  I named him that coz I'm not afraid of death, so you shouldn't be afraid of birth either.

CLEO  Ain't you lucky that you got away with it decades ago.

WINNIE  ...

CLEO  Police guard airports now and dey watch. You should just be glad that none of you lot got put in prison.

WINNIE  Excuse me?

CLEO  No little girl wants to stand up in a court room and say, 'my community did this to me'. But I will.

WINNIE  *(pause)* Is that so? What did I tell you Eve?

CLEO  All dis for pleasing my man yeh? Where's my sexy lace Aunt Winnie? Show me sum handcuffs.

WINNIE  You're a *disgusting* girl.

CLEO  Yes I am. Now please leave me alone. I'm tired.

WINNIE  Is Cleo threatening the community Eve? No I must be hearing things. We'll see about that.

CLEO *holds the doll tightly.* EVE *goes to the kitchen table to start stitching and* WINNIE *leaves.*

## Scene Ten

*Later that evening,* **WINNIE** *enters the bedroom holding straps in her hand whilst* **CLEO** *is sleeping.*

**EVE** *(noticing* **WINNIE***)* Aunt Winnie?

**WINNIE** *stopping* **EVE***, goes by the bed, and begins tying up* **CLEO***.* **CLEO** *wakes up and takes in what is happening.*

**CLEO** Aunt Winnie?!

**WINNIE**

YOU WERE CHOSEN FROM ALL WOMEN AND FOR WOMAN
A SHINING ONE.

**CLEO** What the...

What the fuck? What the fuck is this?

**WINNIE** My broken Angel –

**WINNIE** *exits and takes* **CLEO***'s doll feeling shocked by her own actions.* **EVE** *rushes to the door.*

**WINNIE** *(to* **EVE***)* This is what she brought us to. Cleo cannot keep threatening our community.

**EVE** Aunt Winnie this has gone too far.

**WINNIE** Sit down.

*They both sit down whilst* **CLEO** *continues to shout from the other room.*

**CLEO** Dis is wrong it hurts...tek dis off...tek dis off you nutters... I said tek it off me! Please! Eve! Eve! Please help me! NOW! What I done? Get this crap off me! I ain't kiddin' you knaw. It fuckin' hurts...ahhhh! I'm in pain all over... I'm left with a tiny bullet hole. Now I can't even feel my God damn legs. You sick witches. I'ma scream this place down I swear to God! I can't do this shit! Who the hell are you? You naw!

Naw! You can't do this. I need to be in a clinic! I'm serious. Let me go now! Eve! Eve!

(**WINNIE** *goes to get another plate of eggs and a spoon, hands it to* **EVE** *gesturing to bring it to* **CLEO**)

**CLEO**  Eve?

**EVE** *offers eggs to* **CLEO** *and she refuses and* **EVE** *leaves the plate on the bedside stand.*

**EVE**  I don't blame you Cleo. Nobody wants my eggs. *(Beat)* I'll talk to Aunt Winnie.

## Scene Eleven

*It is morning and* CLEO *is still tied to the bed.* AUNT WINNIE *enters and stands by the doorstep,* EVE *is in the background.*

CLEO  I wanna be cut open!

WINNIE *on doorstep.*

WINNIE  You are open. You're a Queen, but God must touch your wings to protect you. Don't try me just coz you won't accept.

CLEO  Till I orgasm for God, right?

WINNIE  God likes it tight. Even your little doll ain't got it. We ain't suppose to have it.

CLEO  You mek me feel like I'm nothing.

WINNIE  Nothing? But your supposed 'dead' body came back again.

CLEO *spits in* WINNIE*'s face.* EVE *looks at* WINNIE *worried.*

*Pause.*

WINNIE  It's alright. Don't worry. I pushed her.

CLEO *stares at her.*

You wanna be like those fancy models? Going to the doctor's for the knife, mek their breasts bigger. They're left wiv scars too.

CLEO  They choose their gifts.

WINNIE  It's all gifts to please men.

CLEO  Then you better go and pray to your baby boy who never made it to become a man.

*A very long painful pause.*

WINNIE *takes in the comment and leaves.*

*EVE and* CLEO *have an awkward silence and* EVE *comes to untie* CLEO.

You just stood there.

EVE  You shouldn't have said that. It's like her and her baby boy were one soul, all in one belly. Aunt Winnie gets a toothache, the baby would be kicking in her veins. When he died it's like she went along and died with him.

*Beat.*

I don't think I've known anyone so brave.

CLEO  *(struggling to get up)* Brave? I can't breathe sometimes Eve.

EVE  That's what I call brave. You living breathless. I know you might hate me. I guess I'm hiding behind your bravery. About five minutes ago I prayed for my future sins.

EVE *unties* CLEO.

Thank you for showing me.

*Beat.*

CLEO  I'm starving.

EVE  What?

CLEO  I'd like Eve's eggs please.

EVE  I've got something better.

EVE *exits and moments later returns with a bag and starts to bring out the items.*

You never wanted eggs, only apples.

CLEO *goes through the bag.*

CLEO  Apple crunch bars! Eve you joker, you got this.

EVE  Oh and...nothing too fancy but...

*She brings out a miniature bottle of white wine.*

CLEO  You didn't. My favourite. Eve man.

EVE  Knock yourself out.

> CLEO *begins to drink some of the wine.*

> Your hair, it's like a dry forest.

CLEO  Who cares?

EVE  I care and so should your deodorant.

CLEO  I reek don't I?

EVE  Let me get you sum fresh clothes at least.

> EVE *exits to collect some fresh clothes. When back in the kitchen, she spots the red garment and picks it up.*

CLEO  Eve, I'll stink it out.

EVE  Try it on please?

> EVE *goes to help* CLEO *put on the dress.*

CLEO  So where's Kareem at now?

EVE  Freetown. Seein' family.

CLEO  So he's got his secret family out there?

EVE  *(pause)* I don't know.

CLEO  We all have secrets.

> CLEO *is finally in the dress.*

> *Beat.*

EVE  It fits you.

> *Beat.*

CLEO  Police are beggin' women like you and me to come forward.

EVE  Do not get me involved in your drama.

CLEO  Well what makes you think someday *you* won't need what I need right now?

EVE  How dare you?

CLEO  You don't care what happens to me.

EVE  I do, I would give my *world* ya knaw. I would give it to have a baby for myself – for you to have a baby as well.

CLEO  But you won't.

EVE  I mean I would—

CLEO  You *would*— Whatever.

*Beat.*

Come with me to the clinic?

EVE  What?

CLEO  Have the reversal in Paris with me.

EVE  I'm not having this conversation again. I won't.

CLEO  You could save my life and yours, but you won't. You could have the love and the baby you want naturally without the risks and get your senses back, but you won't?

EVE  I would.

CLEO  You would?

EVE  It's your life. I mean that life dat I've been needin' – wantin'.

CLEO  You want my life?

EVE  Yes.

CLEO  You want my scars?

EVE  I have my own scars.

CLEO  You want his dick?

EVE  I need a gift of a baby Cleo!

CLEO  All this for a baby Eve?

EVE  The gift of feelin' me and my baby's heartbeats while in my womb.

CLEO  This is sum sick shit.

EVE  Naw it ain't. So many years I've been walking on eggshells... never doin' or sayin' nothin'. One day yeh, I wanna stomp all over 'em. Dose broken eggshells cut me so – cut me so deeply but dis, dis could be the most beautiful pain I could ever feel!

CLEO  ...

EVE  And I would name my baby girl Cleo.

CLEO  ...And would you have her cut too? Do you hear yourself? I been tired. I need to go somewhere deeper than the Earth...somewhere...somewhere I can feel...my soul... *(A still moment)* He said, 'I need to feel big.' Every poundin took me deep into a place, a place too deep for any man to reach...a place...a place deeper dan the miracle of any womb. He was juss comin' after me, like his piece were hard like CUMING...

EVE *remains standing.*

CLEO  He left me leaking. Both of us leaking...

EVE *comforts her.*

EVE  Shhhh.

CLEO  *(exhaling) I CAN'T BREATHE*!!

EVE  *(she sings tenderly)*
YOU WERE CHOSEN FROM ALL WOMAN AND FOR WOMAN A
    SHINING ONE
My broken Angel.

## Scene Twelve

*It is evening.* EVE *and* CLEO *are asleep in each other's arms in the bedroom.* WINNIE *is awake in the bedroom as if she has been watching them sleep for a while.* EVE *and* CLEO *wake up.*

EVE  ...Cleo's gonna have a bath, get her clothes and we're gonna taxi her to a friend before she goes home. She can leave us now.

WINNIE  Cleo, you're not a man. *You* can carry that desire that's been dormant for so long.

EVE  Naw Aunt Winnie just stop *please.*

WINNIE  I've called Akmid to pick you up.

CLEO  (CLEO *slowly walks towards* WINNIE) But Aunt Winnie... he penetrated...

WINNIE  Get your stuff ready so you can leave. Come on Eve?

EVE *doesn't move.* CLEO *is trying to gain* WINNIE's *attention while* WINNIE *exits.*

CLEO  It was rape Aunt Winnie! He continued while I screamed like a bloody bull!

CLEO *continues towards* WINNIE *as she is about to exit.*

Your baby boy got suffocated at birth and—

WINNIE *dismisses her and* CLEO *continues.*

You won't admit it was your fucking stitches! We're both closed-up but I have the guts to do what you never could and that's why you hate me!

CLEO *then rushes to* EVE.

Eve?

EVE  I...I don't know what to say.

CLEO  Eve?

EVE  Can we take you to a friend—

CLEO  And then what?

EVE  Maybe at least just talk to your husband. You don't need to go back just yet.

CLEO  You're leaving me?

EVE  Clee... I guess he was just making love the way he knew how.

CLEO  You're all the same. I should put you lot in jail! I should put all you fuckers in jail! Of course you would screw me over. You're just a frigid, pathetic virgin who's afraid of a fuck!

EVE  Why don't you have him arrested then, if he raped you?

CLEO  So it's my fault yeh?

EVE  Never said that.

CLEO  Why can't you understand I need to be cut open?!

WINNIE  (offstage yelling) Eve, she's not your lover!

EVE  Can you forgive him?

CLEO  No.

EVE  Can you forgive *me?*

WINNIE  (offstage) Eve! Your work is done!

CLEO  Yes I can. It's not your fault. You're just like your husband, you're a coward.

WINNIE  (coming into the kitchen) Leave that girl alone!

EVE  My heart bleeds for you Cleo.

> EVE *goes to kitchen window hurt and looking outside while* WINNIE *watches her making sure she does not go back in the bedroom.*

CLEO  (she speaks to herself) And I'm done bleeding for you! I'm done bleeding for everyone.

CLEO *sits on the bed and goes into deep thought.* CLEO *then cuddles up in the bed covering herself – noticing the scissors on the bedside table, she reaches for the scissors and decides to physically cut herself underneath her dress and gives a very painful scream and passes out.* WINNIE *and* EVE *are offstage and hear the scream.* EVE *comes back to the bedroom.*

EVE  Cleo!

WINNIE  She's not your problem anymore.

EVE *comes to the bed to* CLEO's *aid and sees the scissors covered with blood.*

EVE  No! Oh my Lord Cleo! Cleo! *(trying to revive her)* My baby! Help me! Help me!

*(to* WINNIE*)* Call the hospital!

*To* CLEO.

I'm getting the ambulance Cleo. Please God help me.

*To* WINNIE.

Give me a chance!

EVE *stays with* CLEO *and* WINNIE *leaves the room.*

## Scene Thirteen

*A year later.* CLEO *walks on and sits down.* EVE *and* WINNIE *are also present on stage behind her but not part of the scene.*

CLEO  I took one bite out da thing, it's just so sweet...juss lookin' at its shape...Lookin' at da apples round like da planet an all dat. *(Beat)* I sat in the park before I got here and I felt a tingle. LOL. Rememberin' Eve teachin' me to be one with the Earth 'n' all dat. It was a chilled-out day, I walked thru da park, letting da sun kiss me, lookin' at the river and my reflection in it, den I realised... I never used to see my reflection... *(Beat)* I gotta paper cut yesterday. When I was a little girl I used to get shit scared of my own blood. Then after the ceremony if I'd cut myself, I wouldn't even notice, but yesterday I didn't panic and I thought of daddy. Don't chat to him no more. It's sad I know. So, Akmid's done a runner. I reckon he's fucked off to Freetown, to be in politics or whatever but that's fine. *(Beat)* I'm cut open now...

I finally got the kind of gift that *Cleo* wanted. Gifts are meant to be opened right? Still feelin' like I'm baptisin' my un-stitched lips when I tek a piss. I'm juss standing there like a born again child whose wet demselves, but I'm a woman now, not a whore.

*Beat.*

I've met a man, a good man, he's proper feelin' me, he's so sweet, he makes me weak at the knees wiv my needs. He baked me an apple pie... I'm finally *'living'*. He gives me butterflies. Butterflies gone ballistic.

I still came here and I find myself amazed by how broken, bent and bullied I allowed myself to be. I try to forget, but it still lives inside me. *(Beat)* There is an Angel of light that makes hope possible. I hope my body and my life are possible. I'm cut open, the hole sees the light. I'm stitch-less, no tightness and though life still squeezes me so tight, I can finally breathe.

So tell me Eve. Have you been cut open too?

*Lights out.*

*Curtain.*

# PROPS

*On kitchen twin shelves*: jars x3, tins x6, shot glasses with flowers x4-5, rice, radio

*On stove*: rag, flat pan, eggs in pan, kitchen utensil for eggs, kitchen utensil rack

*On table*: tray with plate, fork, napkin, eggs and toast, plastic or enamel plate, african basket, crochet, scissors, needle cushion with thread, magazines, plastic table cloth
Chairs x2

*On side table*: toast x2, napkins, tea kettle, small bin, apples in a basket, sugar lumps, tea biscuits, PG tea

*Shelves top table*: light, light bulbs, cup with forks and small spoons, drinking cups and tea cups, post letter case, bracelets in box, box for bracelet, phone, can opener, vase, flower, water bottles

*On visible back shelves*: cups, plates, bottles, jars, super malt & lucozade, cans, vodka bottle, mango juice, coconut juice, broom and dust pan

*Hidden shelves*: dolls/stuffed animals, small cans, big cans, small cans, bottle of palm oil, shopping bag (EVE) with apple crunch and mini bottle wine, wine refill, jug for punch, punch refill, bag with lingerie, red vulgar lingerie, handcuffs, flower blossom

*Backstage*: bench, belly, EVE jacket, EVE shoes, strap, blood

*Side table*: african hanging decorative cloth, cup of water, light bulbs, lamp

*Stool:* red dress

*Bed*: mattress, pillow, pillow case and mattress cover, bed sheet, tissue box, scissors, doll, african pillow on floor

CLEO – jacket
CLEO – shoes
CLEO – shopping bag with junk and apples

# THIS
# IS
# NOT
# THE
# END